CACTUS SWEATER

CACTUS SWEATER

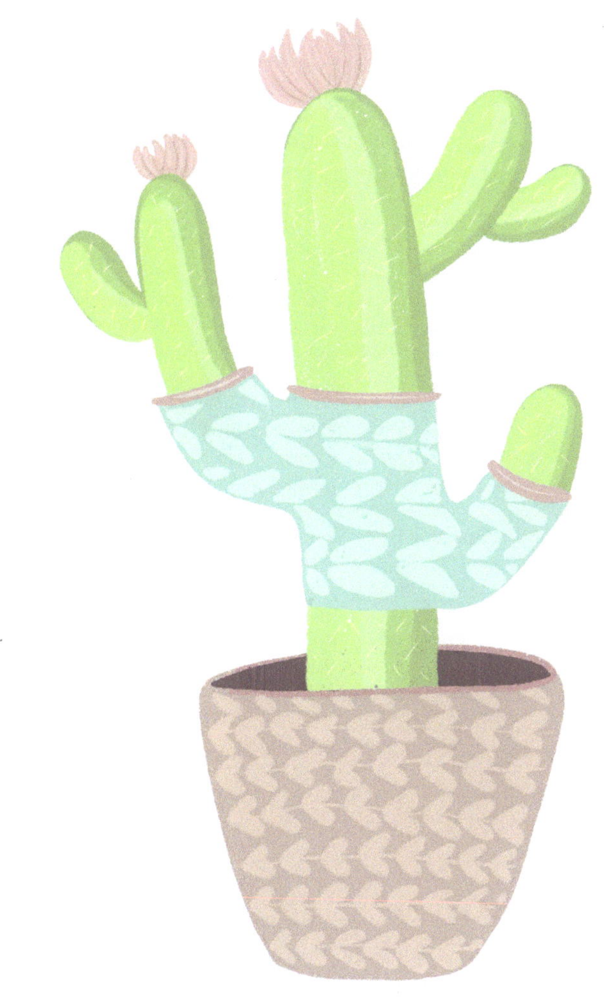

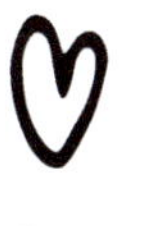

Dune Stewart

Published by Dune Stewart

Book Design by Kory Kirby

Illustrations by Maryam Abbas

ISBN 978-1-7351015-1-4

Printed in the United States of America

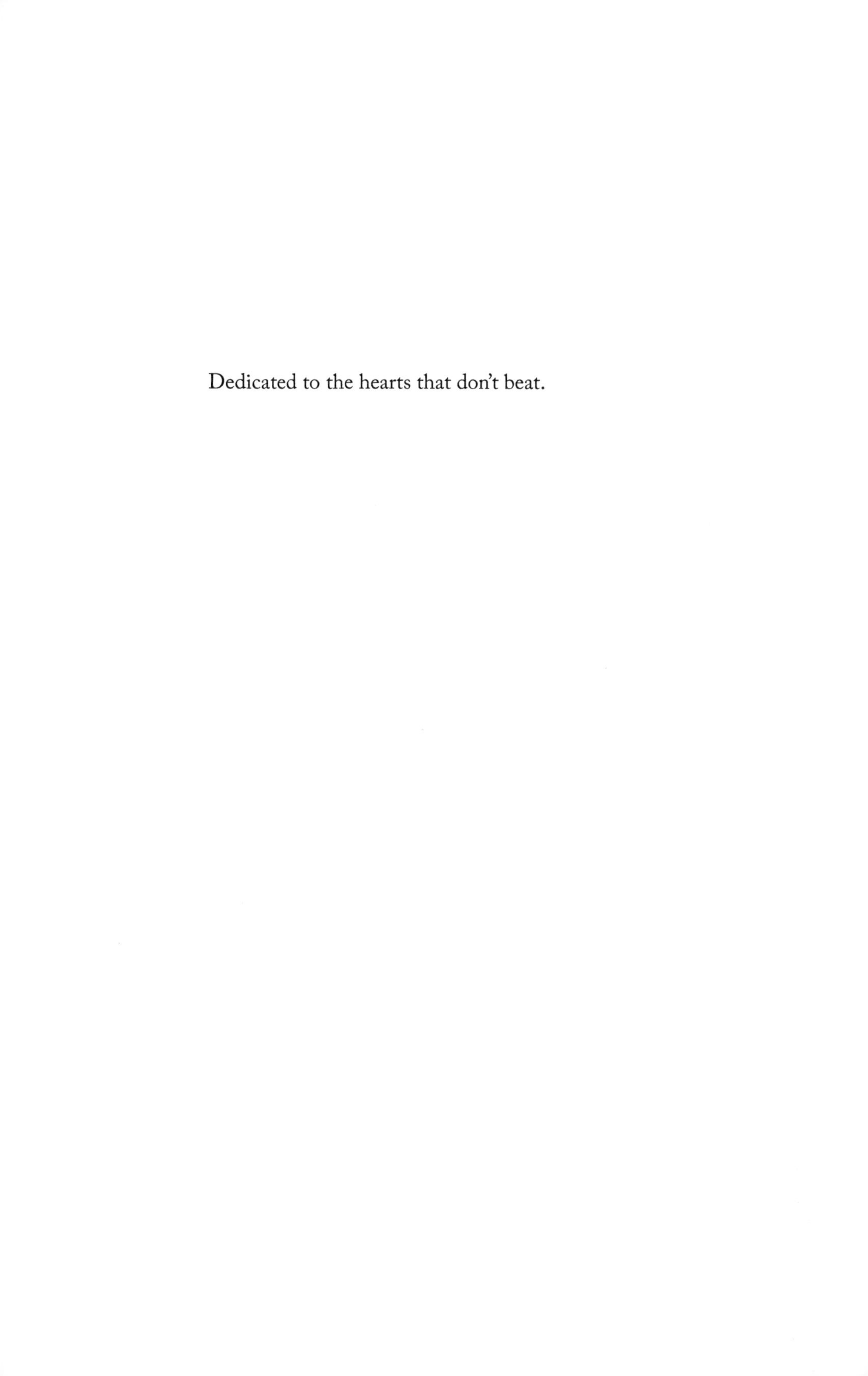

Dedicated to the hearts that don't beat.

Contents

The sweetest revenge is not a life well lived.
The sweetest revenge, is revenge.

I think I never knew when I was going to be ready to start this. I think I was always waiting for the right person to come along, and maybe I would know from the amount of moments we shared that it would finally be the time to begin this next journey in my life. I guess it's because I never trusted my instincts, and that's why I never felt it was the right time to start. Many events have occurred over the past few days, seeing people lose their lives, as if "dropping like flies" were an understated metaphor. At first, I was numb to the occasion, since it felt like I have always dealt with death as a neighbor, always knocking at my door until I am ready to invite it in for dinner. Now, it makes me critically question how I choose to live my life.

Not in a sense of—

Panicking with anxiety, scraping at the walls for answers to deaf tones of faraway screams—

Rather, the motivation for the continuous search to find what fills my life.

What makes me the most happy is when I wake up in the morning with a cup of coffee and a husky dog.

With all my heart, I want to believe you're the answer. You may not see it, but I sure as hell feel it.

Maybe, because I love you…

Love?

I've been trying to figure out what love means, and how to identify its contradiction with lust. I am trying to decide whether it's the loneliness that distorts my vision of you, or if my inexperience with love has me second-guessing its presence. I often think about how there is no cure for my disorder, but how when I am with you, all of the symptoms disappear, and I am just focused on you.

I think about how:

I go through ups & downs constantly, but you're always there experiencing them with me.

I wake up with the same disorder, and also with the same thoughts of you.

When I am up, you are always the person I want to talk about.

When I am down, my hands don't crave a gun, but instead crave your grasp.

If this was just lust, then I could easily let you go like the drug habits I've had for five years, but instead—

I found a better drug to replace them.

And let me tell you,

I'm addicted.

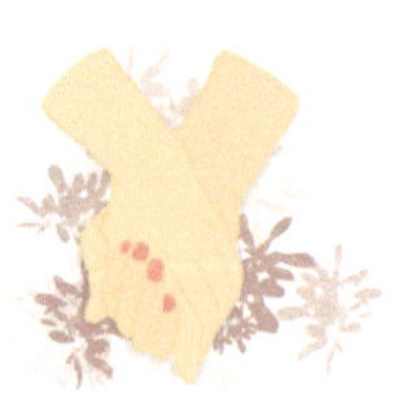

Poetry is, in all forms—

Love.

It carries the word in a spiral,
allowing independent morphing of context,
bringing light and darkness to a gray gradient wall,
knowing it can destroy or heal anything in its wake.

This spiral has recently destroyed my present,
creating a dark box,
so I can't see what may lie ahead for a glimmer of hope.

And so I press on,
up the spiral,
in search of some light in this darkness.

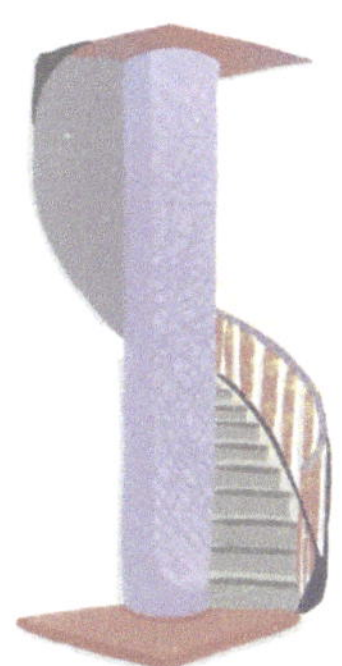

Now and Then

When I see your name appear,
butterflies turn
to heavy stone,

weighing on me.

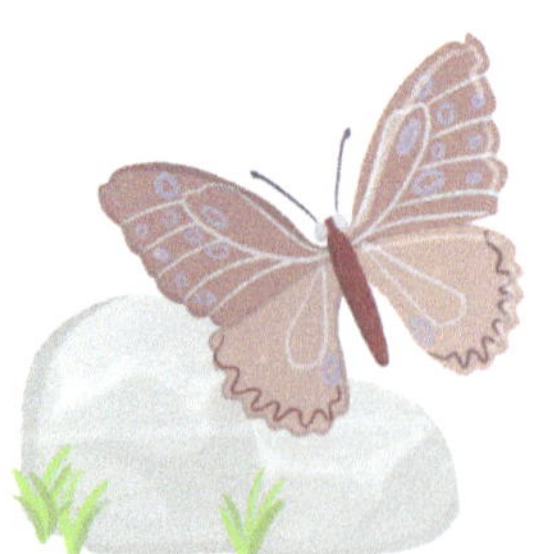

Smirk

Remember that smirk?

I always dream of it.

The slight tilt of your face as you nod

after you gaze into the ball pit of emotions showering from my heart to my eyes—

the way your laugh slips through the spaces of your teeth as your hair sways from side to side.

Right now,
you're lit by two fires—
one that lights your portrait,
and another that attempts to fuel the visual abyss of your pupils.

I am in the perfect moment, or am I just dreaming again?

Do You Recall—

When I kissed your hand,
and said

Let me be yours forever?

When I kissed your cheek,
and remarked

Your eyes glisten like the moonlight
that gives starlight to the night sky?

When I kissed you—

and you were left—

speechless?

Lips

My lips:

a pardon to your hand,
a suction to your cheek,
a dream for your lips.

Your lips:

a sweet cherry red,
setting the stage ablaze,
leaving my lips
applauding for their performance.

Come Here

I want our noses to bridge under one another,
leaving only space for the smell of love,
and the motion of lust
that tells our lips why we stay superglued.

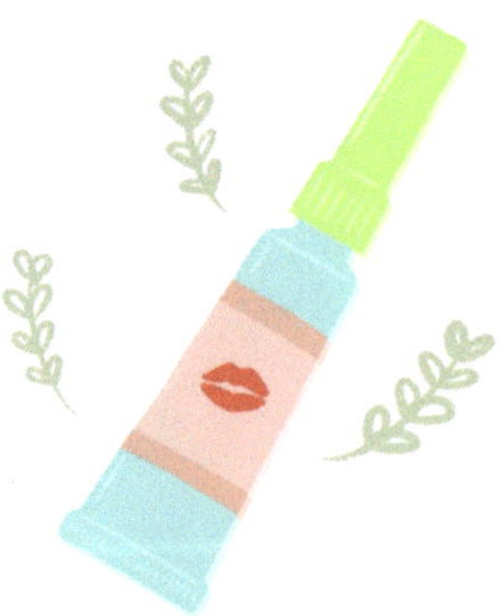

O' Sweet Lavender

My nickname for you
would be lavender.

It is the sweetest of all smells,
the aroma from my coffee mug,
the plant of Life.

It stands taller in unison,
swaying over to a curl that conveys:

Smell me
O' Smell me,

Let our beautiful souls intertwine
into the sky to show the clouds
why they are not worthy to be
considered an entrance to Heaven,
for our scents
intertwine with perfect chemistry,
intoxicated with love.

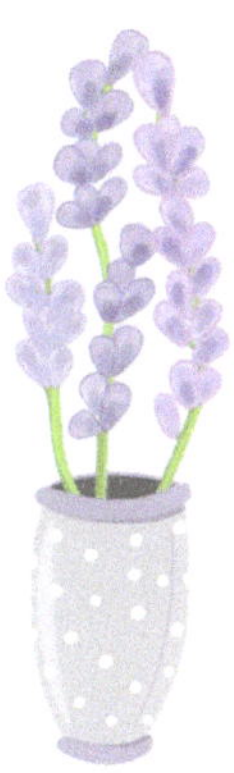

Stay with Me

I just want to cuddle with you,
so I know how time is relative.

To know how one hold
can combine two spirits.

How warmth is collaborative,
and how matches creates fire.

How our feet form the stems of our legs,
so the roses can blossom with our kiss.

For when our eyes close,
I can see you perfectly.

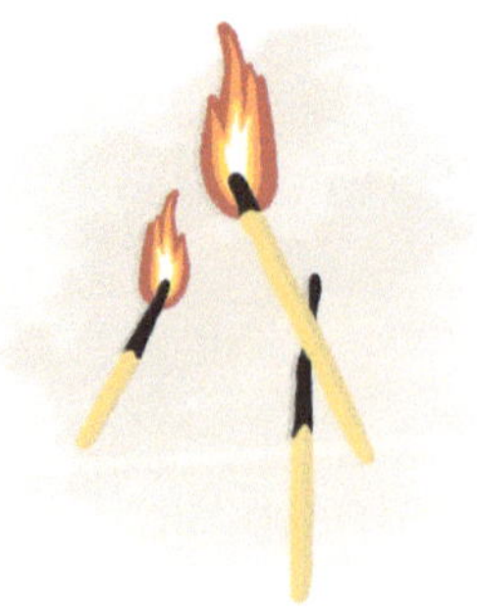

Kiss

The soft touch of your skin
mirrors silk.

Your gaze back at me
speaks infinitely.

Your lips,
sweet juicy cherries.

Your tongue with mine,
a cherry-stem knot.

Substance of You

Substance abuse,
not a stranger to us two.
Drugs aren't the most dangerous,
but I have craved an addiction:
You.

The smoke that fills my lungs
exhales laughter and tears that I can't feel sober,
while everything I drink fogs my mind's clutter,
leaving me dazed in front of you.

The way I gaze into your eyes,
without a joint or bottle in hand,
to remind me why life is worth living—

here,

with you.

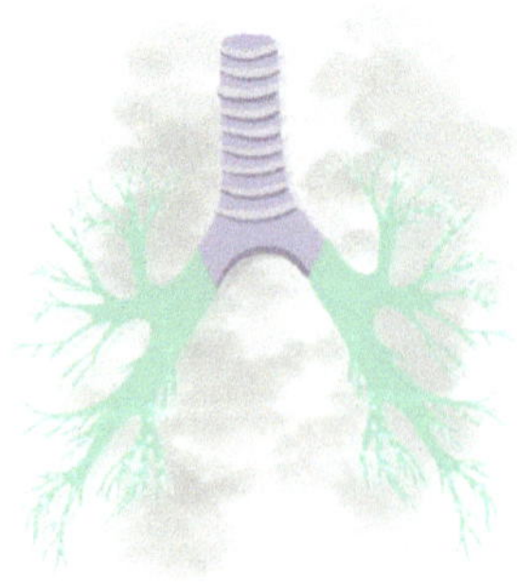

Why

Is it love or determination that draws me to you?
Maybe a little of both.

What drives my mind to see you

tilt
your
head

with that cute smirk?

It must be your teeth…
or your eyes,

I can't decide.

Why can't this blossom into the spring I see?
Is it the winter blues or the fall leaves that keeps you questioning?

Let me be the sun,
and you the moon.

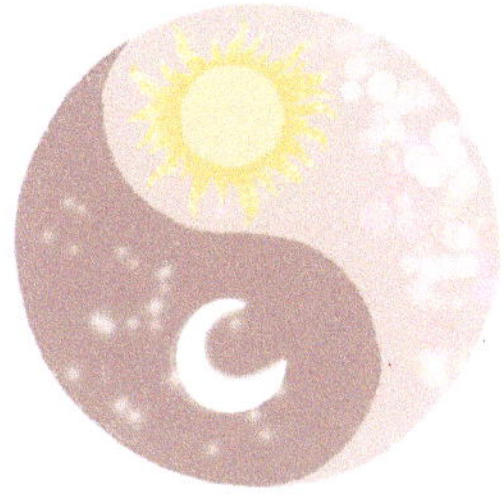

Profit

How do you profit?
Through money and greed,
or through happiness and laughter?

As a child,
I was taught that money was sweeter than life itself,
always making your teeth shine brighter in the day,
buying all your needs with a wink of an eye.

As an adult,
I learned money is the childhood nightmare,
where evil lurks in its grasp,
and happiness is not paid forward with paper,
but with hands.

Yours caressing mine,
mine caressing yours,
a profit so powerful to gain
that green paper looks more like shrubs.
Our hands the shears,
deciding what it'll look like to us.

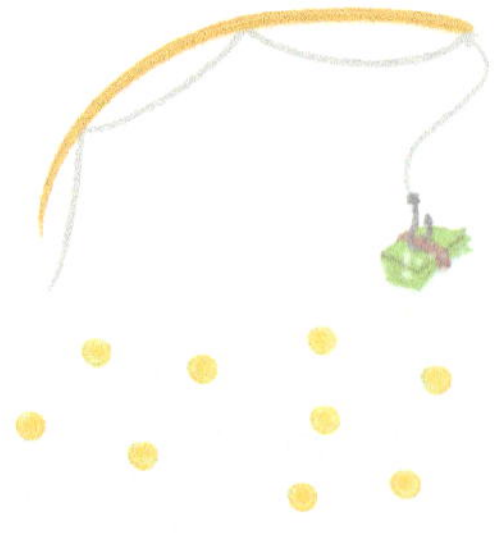

In This Moment

You don’t have to love me.

I just want us to hold each other tight,
letting go of who we are,
being
spirits that tango to the hummingbird’s tune,

where your heartbeat soothes my anxiety,
and your arms cradle the comfort my soul craves.

You don’t have to love me,

but just know that I do.

The World

Other offers cannot compare,
for I know who truly cares,
but why can't you see
that for you,
I offer a limitless world?

One where expectations meet reality.

Look and See

Both of us can look,
but only one of us can see.

You look and see us,
but I only see you.

You look with caution,
I see the potential.

You look confused,
I see enlightenment.

You look for the answer,
I see the solution.

If We Could Become Us

I want to show you:

how the world has a universal language,
why the ocean chases us when we tease our presence,
what a rose means when it holds itself up,
when timing is not important,
where if you are willing to wait,

you'll believe in fate.

I Miss Us

I miss when we were friends.
Now estrangement defines your side of the bed.

Your imprint left in the side of my mind
questions why my starfish pose
seems neglected in the ocean of softness.

The part of me that exists beyond what I control,
how I act,
no matter how valiant and superior,
it always seems to be—

not enough.

I guess it's always hard to match perfection.

What Is It Worth?

If I let go,
would you grab me?

Would your clutch be enough to sustain this rubber band that keeps us swaying into each other's presence, but not enough to hold us together?

Would the hand you use be grasped by a stronger force of its counterpart to scream for its victory—

to beseech the Gods to withhold a presence from its taking?

Would you hold on,
or would you let it go,
as fast as you're letting all of this—

us—

go?

Forever

You want me in your life forever,
and I want you to be my forever.

Too bad it's not always interchangeable.

As a Friend

You say you love me so much

yet I'm the only one pouring my heart into this.

You say as friends.

I say you're just scared.

But I can't have you NOT in my life.

Then how much does this mean to you?
Not enough apparently.

But… I love you—
as a friend.

To My Best Friend

I go through days and nights constantly changing my perception of how I feel about you. Most days I'm enthralled with the idea of being around you, and other days I'm sad, because I know it doesn't exist how I wish it to be. Regardless, every day I awake and lay to rest thinking of you.

Some days I feel resentment, because your words don't clarify your actions, and it's confusing. I feel as though I am a safety net, and I'm here as a guarantee, in case you fall. It feels like if I win, it won't be because I won, it will be because you let it happen.

It sucks waking up, wanting to talk to you about everything, and knowing neither of us can. I see us growing distant from the circumstances of us both being uncomfortable with where this has gone, and it pains me to say, I am losing my best friend.

You say you can't live without me, yet, you're hesitant to give us a chance, as if the status quo is eternally stable. We're both slipping away, and I don't know what to do about it anymore.

Sincerely,

A Remorseful Stranger

Magic 8 Ball

Magic 8 Ball…

Do you think this relationship will work out?
Don't count on it.

Will I ever feel the reciprocal love I give to her?
Very doubtful.

Is she the one?
Outlook not so good.

Should I just move on from this never-ending nightmare?
Signs point to yes.

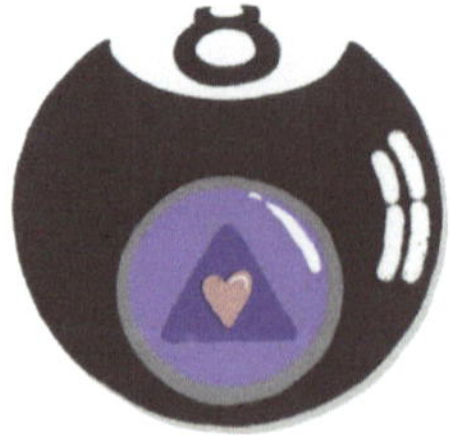

Tug-of-War

On one side,
I am struggling.
pulling two ends of a rope,
self-defeating,
exhausted.

On the other side,
I see
a wound rope clutched,
pulled mighty

with a smile
that says:
You were never going to win.

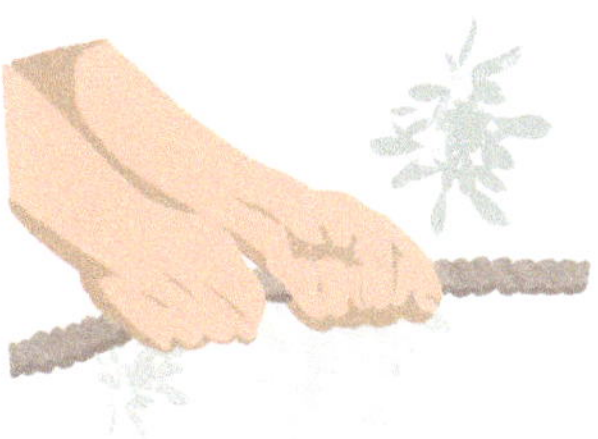

Silly Rabbit

You had me believe
you were Alice.

Took me into the rabbit hole,
where dreams and fantasy become reality,
and that gentle voice had reassurance.

When I woke up from this dream,
I realized you were never Alice,
you were Trix,
and played me to be a gullible kid.

Spirit

The time we spend
fills me with butterflies
but by the end of the night
The wings are ripped off.

To you,
I am a whisper to the wind,
a voice in the air that you ignore,
and you blew out my spirit
like it was your birthday wish.

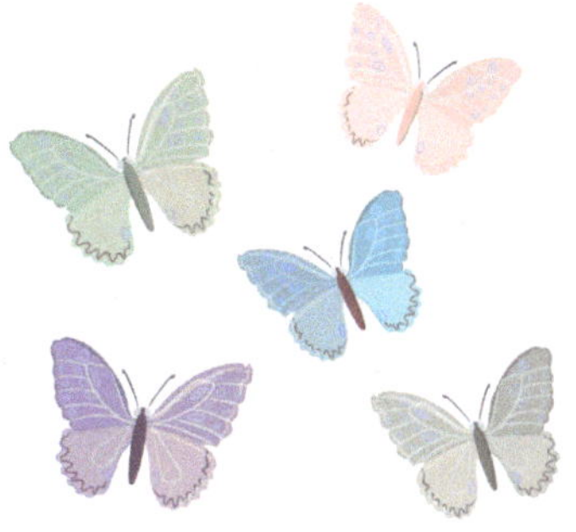

Naive

Is it you playing me
or
you playing yourself?

Am I to believe naivety
is threaded with just ignorance
or bullshit lies as well?

Your words shatter hearts
and your soul smells sour.
The gestures you make are so welcoming
they're threatening.

Wait
I know who you are.

Poison ivy.

The Hate You Give

—Is like mud,
sticky enough to pull me down
but kind enough to also let me go with just a few marks.

The resistance is poison ivy wrapped to form my coffin,
spitting with acid:

I shall drag you even when you lie dead in my wake.

With the assurance that,
no—
you don't love me.

Yet here I stand,
still,
waiting for you to accept this love I give.

Shredded Paper Thin

Tear the screen to sheets of unsung love.
Let the projector run a blank white light
with no home movies to display.

Let the emotional abuse show onto the blank canvas
since each heartbreaking word
left me speechless—

shredded.

A paper with words ready to be laid
onto its surface.
A story that knows its course,
but you wrote the other path.

While you trek along,
can you see, between the border of trees—
me,
walking parallel,
hoping our paths still meet again
even after all you've put me through?

Indecisive

A rose's thorn
pricks the blood
dripping into an abyss
of an unknown conclusion.

Where does it seep?
Where does it evaporate?
Where does it live?

Answering Questions with Questions

No Man's Land

In the crossfire,
blazing lights are alluring,
but I caution you to listen to where they land…

To how the words you speak,
the actions you make,
Create victims of your crimes
That leave a bigger scar than the bullet on their chest.

You will see a hollow emptiness that begs to surround their worthiness of existence.

We are not defined by what happens to us,
and although the emotions that follow are toiling,
just remember—

Karma's a bitch,
especially when the gun gets jammed.

Climax

Something most readers look forward to in their book—

Ours?

Just a conflict,

with no resolution.

Cactus Sweater

A prickly pear
has penetrated this beautiful sweater you've sewn.

The threads have sharpened to needles,
and what I believed to be comforting
now sticks me with many holes,
deflating this water-balloon corpse
that you so wish to see turn into a puddle—

left standing,
a reservoir,
for the needles to grow into its shell.

A cactus

that wears its victims' clothes,
complacent and content in its stature,
knowing it has destroyed a beautiful presence,
but is unscathed from its crime.

Why does this beautiful sweater you've sewn
still look so warm,
even after its been torn and ripped
by the ugliness you've shown?

My mind says let it be trash,
but my heart craves its dangerous warmth.

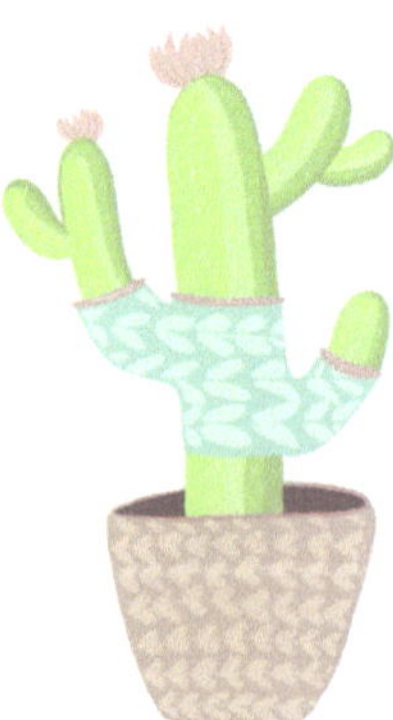

Time

You agree with me that time is precious
and life is so valuable.

Then why do you like to waste mine?

Sweet Sucker Kiss

As I lay crying into your shoulder,
the one you kept steady for those defeated by your broadsword,
you kissed my forehead.

Did you care to heal the wounds you tore open,
or the ones you made for yourself in battle,
pretending you were the victim?

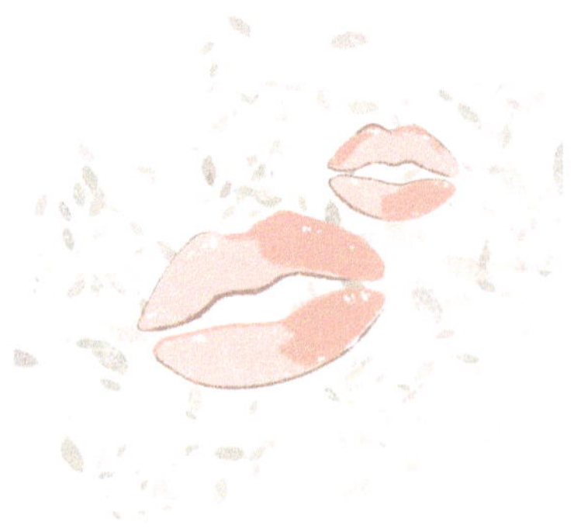

Lust and Love

At first it was love from a blindfold,
now it's lust.

For the starlight in your eyes
was just my own reflection,
and your black pupil
was a sign of self-rejection.

The tears you weep
are black ink,
unremovable from my pores,
but that's because I let you lay into me,
the way I am laying into you now.

The End of Us

I just want to capture the essence of beauty
without lying
when really I'm just trying
to make a definition for myself.

The second you question
it's endgame
never feels the same
what used to be blood in your veins
is now taken in vain.

What this became
is a runaway train
where two paths merged to one
but now I forgot this was supposed to be fun.

It's late
and after we enter the door
the only thing out of our mouth is hate
and I feel I have to leave
before this house sells at probate.

It's sad to see
but it's a part of life
and I'm here for the journey
not the light in sight.

Play Time Is Over

A toy for a little girl's pleasure.

The string on my back continues to thread through my system
like my voice is muffled under the words you speak,
trying to scream

LET ME OUT!

But does anybody ever hear the screams?
Maybe I'm just a product,
a toy to be played with and put to the side.
Laugh and joke together,
until you get tired…

Tired of playing with me,
like the garbage in the side of your room.
Pick me up when you get bored?

Sounds like a problem for you and not for me.
Wake me up from this ridiculous dream.
This girl can't be seriously toying with me
expecting everything to be okay and for me to be—

by your side like I'm supposed to be.

An Instrument

I'm just an instrument,
nothing to say,
only strings for you to play.

Am I a piano,
so I can pretend like I know the key to your heart,
or am I a guitar with strings to your game?

Ripped apart.

Just a bare instrument now,
thought I was safe to be,
turns out you knew how to make a melody.

Thinking no strings attached
was a playdate for two,
and I was left falling in love with you.
But that date's over
and now you focus on the beat,
leaving my crumpled-up body in the streets.

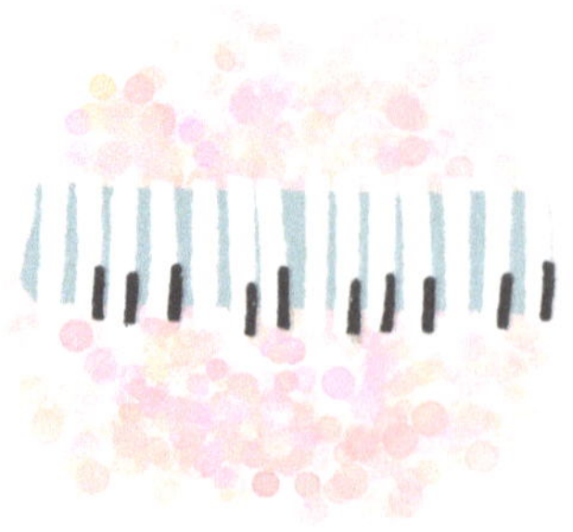

You don't want me to go
because I carry the sorrows he creates for you,
and there's no one else there to pick up the pieces
like the person you broke in two.

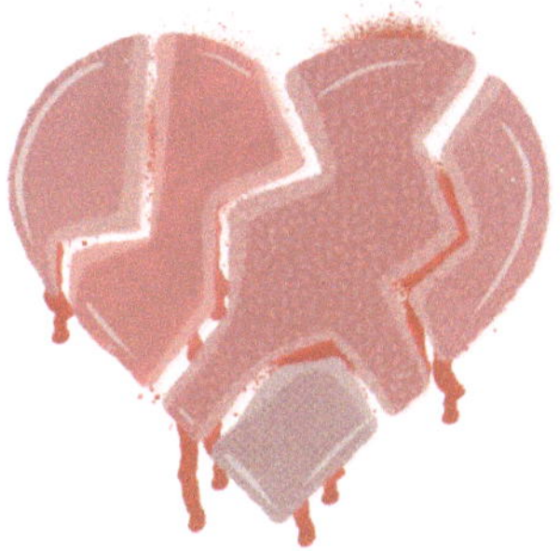

What Are We, now?

You said you can't leave him
and you can't lose me,
so I archive the issue
as a memory to remember,
not an agency to resent.

This dark trench of no clear path
leads me second guessing its worth,
like if I walk far enough to reach you,
would it have been worth the struggle I endured?

Would the mud and dirt on my new shoes
understand why I kept them in the quicksand soil,
or would they resent me

like I resent you?

iRobot

Everything I used to love about you,
I can't stand.

Your positivity oozed appreciation,
now it's a facade.

You look for the best in situations,
I say you're not dynamic enough.

I'm here to date a person,
not a robot.

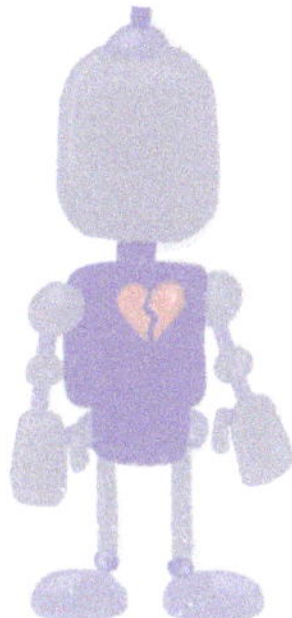

The difference between then and now
is I was blind
to see how you could turn

Fine Ass

into multiple meanings—

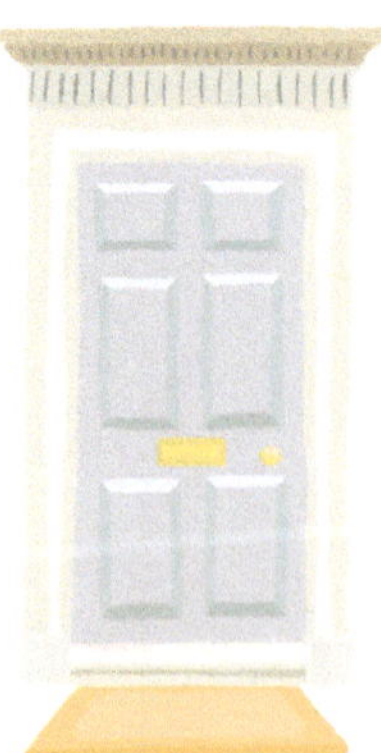

Doormat

Soaking wet
from the soles of the shoes carrying
the people you decide to walk over.

Wiping aggressively
to make sure our voices don't enter your comfort zone,
where your weapons are left at the door
and you can pretend you did nothing wrong.

When it gets wet,
it gets moldy,
and after so many souls laid onto the rusty spikes,
you'll blame us for the smell,
when you are the one who dragged all of us through the mud.

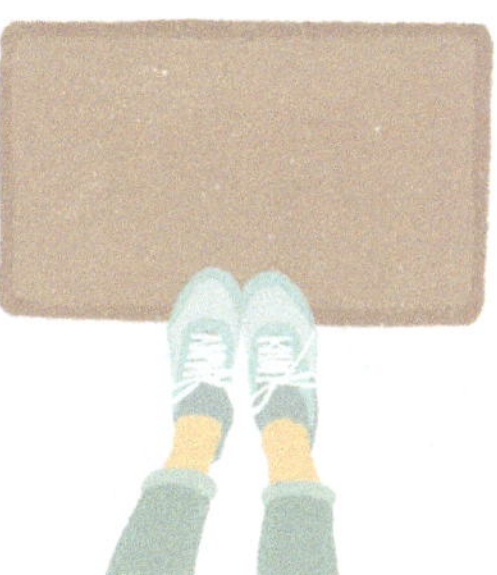

My Condolences

I apologize for the hurt you feel.

It must be hard being alone.

I know that feeling all too well.

You say it's really bad.

So, I pick up my shattered pieces
and piece enough together to help a person feel welcome,
but my cracked super-glue mirror is no match
for the stones you cast so forcefully
my way.

I should have expected it.

You say it's bad and you've never felt so alone,
but dear,
don't you see?

My history is not equivalent to your petty crimes.
I've seen too much to know this is all you mean to say.
It's pathetic.
Your apology is pathetic.
This love I had for you—
                                        feels pathetic.

Tell me…

Does the eyeliner you put on need to be waterproof?

I wasn't sure if monsters could cry.

Does the hair you straighten stay healthy?

I wasn't sure if everything you burn gets healed.

Does your fingers burn at the touch?

I wasn't sure if your match tips were drenched in kerosine.

But I guess what I really wanted to ask is…

Do you carry around a scythe?
Because everything I see you grab ahold of dies in your presence
and you leave it with a smile.

Stranglehold

A sharp lace
that hung, a thread of possibility,
was grabbed by claws
and strangled me to death,
to know what it was like
to take someone's breath away.

Garrote Wire

Buried

Talking to you is more stressful than finishing my college degree.
I gave up substance abuse but grab my beer and weed,
because this is going to be a long night
shuffling through the weak words
put together to put this bullshit to rest.
I'm just tired of how it always seems that you think I'm available for you,
every day of the week.

Don't you notice you ripping at my seams,
like—

It's okay,
he always comes through for me.
You'll see,
he's the best friend I could never be—

I just pity how spiteful this gets.
You play yourself like you played me,
except this time we're in the same dream,
and you're clutching onto me for advice,
while I just let go and you scream,
and leave you to the burdens you bury for yourself.

If you thought I was going to hold onto you,
you were mistaken.

I guess you can call me Billie,
because I just buried a friend.

Death Certificate

You say you're woke
but the next time I see you
it'll be a wake
from digging your own grave

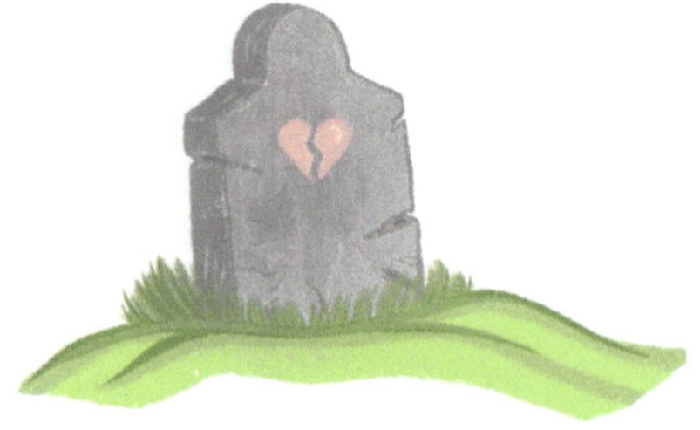

Trust

I trust you can keep a secret,
but I don't trust you can keep it in your pants.

Maybe a friend,
definitely not a lover.

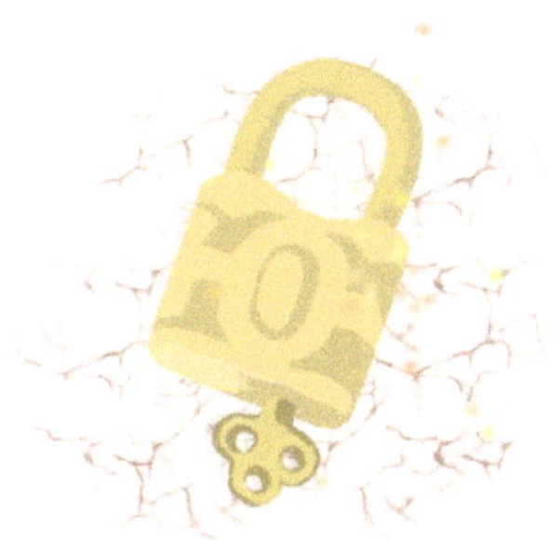

Thank You

Without you,
with us not being We,
I've come to find myself again.

I have come to say fuck you,
and thanks.

Now I exercise,
go to therapy,
write more,
read more,
and distance myself from you.

The journey was worth it.

Wool Sweater

After thread and needle became one:
destructive.
I yearned for a sweater more warm.

One that I could ask what it was made of,
because it was so soft,
always comforting.

Was it linen,
Was it silk,
Was it wool?

It caresses my body to know my worth.
The joy we bring each other
deserves a place on a hanger,
but I'm too busy showing it off to the world.

I forgot your pricks shadowed in the depth of my closet,
scraping against the surface when I open to your presence,
with sharp points threatening me to gaze into your wake.

But with every new flower blossomed,
there is spring,
and spring cleaning
is just right around the corner.

The End of a Road

Here in this moment,
I hear pages of a book flipping by,
peaceful wind.

The love I yearn to give
was not yet for me to receive,
but my vision is no longer foggy
with daylight seeping through its transparent curtain
to reveal a beautiful flower.

This time it is not a rose,
where its thorns can prick the sweater I want to call
home.
It is a single flower petal,
also looking for its new place in the world,
And I ~~think~~
(hope)
it's going to be with me.

Reminder

I was reminded
of how we could only focus on
one thought at a time,
and how
this
would only be temporary.

I was reminded
of how I lived my life last year,
and you never came up once.

I know I'll be fine now.

Goodbye//Good Riddance

Fin

What hurts more—
is knowing how easy it is to let go.

Like,
love can just vanish
in
seconds

while memories become—

distant thoughts
turning to misfortune,
ending the chapter.

Re-dedicated to those who took their power back.

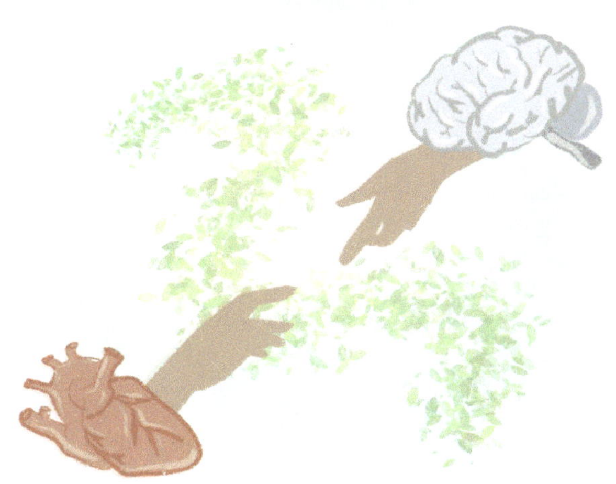

"Don't let mistreatment change who you are. You should never be someone's second choice. Just say goodbye, and move on to find somebody worth your time."

Cactus Sweater Playlist

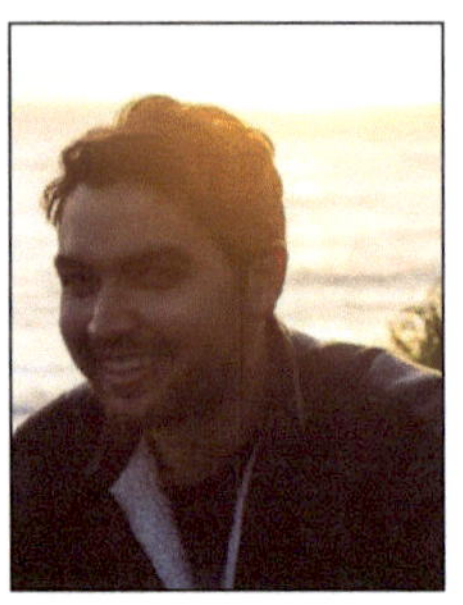

Dune Stewart is a multi-faceted freelance photographer and writer, striving to produce work that resonates with people around the world. He recently produced a photo book titled, *Premonition*, that surrounds the stages of the COVID-19 experience in the United States, which is apart of his upcoming solo show exhibition. He graduated from Arizona State University with a BFA in Photography. He is also the host of the podcast, *Do You Like Ice Cream?* - An Artist Podcast, where he interviews artists across the globe, to pinpoint their uniqueness in the multitude of artistic crafts. His other interests include: voice acting, Twitch streaming, hip-hop music, and filmmaking. This is his second poetry book. His first book, *A Journey of Perspective* can be found on Amazon.

To learn more about him, visit:
dunestewartphotography.com
facebook.com/dunestewart
instagram.com/dunestewart
twitter.com/dunejacob
twitch.tv/R2DUNE2
www.youtube.com/DUNEJACOB

www.ingramcontent.com/pod-product-compliance
Lightning Source LLC
LaVergne TN
LVHW052308100826
845147LV00006B/707